The Ten Most Expensive Tax Mistakes...

...that cost Real Estate Agents Thousands

Paul Dion CPA CTC

The Ten Most Expensive Tax Mistakes
That Cost Real Estate Agents Thousands

Paul Dion CPA CTC

Visit our website at **www.StillwaterPress.com** for more information.

First Stillwater River Publications Edition

ISBN-10: 0-692-31966-2
ISBN-13: 978-069231-966-6

CONTACT: Paul Dion CPA CTC
22 West Street, Suite 6, Millbury, MA 01527
(508) 853-3292, (401) 490-3193 www.pauldioncpa.com

1 2 3 4 5 6 7 8 9 10
Licensed through an agreement with William T. Zumwalt CPA
Cover design by Dawn M. Porter
Published by Stillwater River Publications, Glocester, RI, USA

LIABILITY DISCLAIMER: The material contained in this book is general in nature and is not intended as specific advice on any particular matter. The author and publisher expressly disclaim any and all liability to any persons whatsoever in respect of anything done by any such person in reliance, whether in whole or in part, on this book. Any services, references, and/or websites that may be mentioned or referred to in this book are provided for information purposes only. Please take appropriate legal or professional advice before acting on any information contained in this book.

Table of Contents

Introduction

I'm not a gambler, but I will bet you this:

You pay too much at tax time.

Why is that a bet I'm willing to make? The easy answer is I have tons of evidence on my side: For over twenty years I've helped our clients reduce their tax burden by developing easy to follow plans that result in the lowest *legal* tax liability possible.

Why the emphasis on the word *legal?* As a business owner you often can choose to complete and record a transaction by more than one method. The IRS and the courts back up your right to choose the option that results in the lowest legal tax liability. (If you don't believe me, believe ex-Chief Justice William Rehnquist, who once said, "There is nothing wrong with a strategy to avoid the payment of taxes. The Internal Revenue Code doesn't prevent that.")

In other words, the IRS and the courts fully support your right to be *smart*. In this case, being smart means avoiding taxes whenever possible.

Keep in mind tax *avoidance* planning is perfectly legal. Tax *evasion* – paying lower taxes by lying, cheating, or just plain being sneaky – is not. You just have to know steps to ensure you run your business the smart way.

Don't worry – we'll help you.

The other reason I'm confident you're paying too much at tax time is because understanding the ins and outs of ever-changing tax laws is a full-time job. As a real estate agent, your main focus – and rightly so – is on marketing properties, developing leads, building long-term relationships with lenders and appraisers and title companies… in short, doing all the things that let you list and sell as many homes as possible. You put all your energy into closing deals because doing *that* puts money in your pocket. You shouldn't expect or even *want* to be a tax planning expert.

Tax planning is what *we* do best. We can't sell houses, but we can help you put more money in your pocket by reducing your taxes. We'll do what *we* do best so you can do what *you* do best… and you'll make more money in the process. The key? Following a simple plan that ensures you don't leave money on the table.

Here's a quick example. Say last year you grossed $60,000. Well done, by the way – the average *median family* income in the U.S. is around $50,000. To make the math easy, we'll pretend that 30% of your gross went to taxes and Social Security. (If you're one of our clients, you paid less.) That means out of the $60,000 you earned, only $42,000 ended up in your pocket.

What if I could show you, using perfectly legal and time-tested tax planning strategies, how to keep an additional $2,000, $4,000, or more in your pocket? Without working more hours, making dramatic changes to your daily routine... or even selling another house or two?

It's not an empty promise. The key is to avoid the ten most expensive tax mistakes real estate agents – and millions of other business owners and self-employed individuals – make.

So let's dive in!

Mistake #1
Failing to Plan

Granted, the above is not a sexy title – but work with me.

For a lot of people, sitting down with their accountant at tax time may feel a little like the movie *Groundhog Day*, where Bill Murray's character finds himself living the same day over and over again. You weed through your receipts and reports and do the best you can… but waiting until tax time to do tax *planning* is like closing the barn door after the horses have run away.

No matter how hard your accountant tries, if you didn't know you could write off your son's braces as a business expense and plan effectively to take advantage of the write-off… it's too late.

And you lost money.

So let's take a step back. As a real estate agent, no matter how many houses you sell or how much money you make, *you are a business.* Money flows in and out of your business in three basic ways: As gross income, as expenses, and as taxes. Simple, right? Income, minus expenses, minus taxes, equals your net income (and net income is the money in your pocket.)

How do you increase net income? There are two basic ways. (Don't worry: Accounting 101 will be finished in a minute. This brief accounting discussion lays the groundwork for every tax planning strategy that follows.)

First, you can *increase* your income: Listing more properties, selling more homes, serving as an advisor to real estate investors, etc. In sports terms, increasing income is like being on offense: You work hard to put more points on the board.

You can also increase net income by *decreasing* your expenses and your taxes. In sports terms that's like playing defense: You take steps to keep your opponents – in this case, your expenses and the IRS – from putting more points on the board. Cutting expenses can and does pay off, but for most real estate agents taxes are a bigger expense. And besides, you can cut your marketing spending… but what if that causes you to sell fewer homes? In the long run a short-term savings may mean you make less money overall – and who wants that?

The taxes you pay, on the other hand, do not benefit you in *any* way. (They benefit the government, but that's another issue.) You and I can sit and evaluate the pluses and minuses of trading in your vehicle for a hybrid car and whether the tax benefits and fuel savings offset the time value of money of your down payment and the increase in car payments… but if you pay $1,000 less in taxes, there's *no* evaluation necessary.

Paying less in taxes is a *good* thing. *Period.*

Plus, smart tax planning *guarantees* results. If you decide to spend two more hours each week networking with other real estate professionals, you *hope* the time you spend pays off in the long run – but there's no guarantee it will. On the other hand, if together we set up a medical expense reimbursement plan and deduct the cost of your son's braces, you are *guaranteed* to save money.

Bottom line, it only makes sense to take the bird in the hand over the two birds in the bush. (And the great thing is that effective tax planning could free up more money to spend chasing some of those birds in the bushes.)

So let's take a further step back. Many people simply collect all their receipts, turn them in at tax time, and hope their accountant can "do something" with an unwieldy stack of papers. Planning requires knowledge, so let's take a second to ensure you know whether a particular expense is likely to be deductible.

Here are some of the average real estate agent's most common deductible expenses, in alphabetical order (I'm an accountant – it's my job to make sure things are in order):

- Advertising
- Bank fees on business accounts
- Benefits (health care, etc)
- Car and truck expenses
- Commissions and fees
- Depreciation
- Dues (trade associations and business-related organizations)
- Gifts to customers, service suppliers, etc
- Insurance (health, liability, etc)

- Legal, accounting, and professional services
- Meals and entertainment
- Office expenses (including supplies)
- Pension and retirement plans
- Rent or lease expense
- Repairs and maintenance
- Services performed by independent contractor
- Travel expenses
- Utilities
- Wages

  Everything on the list above is an expense you pay using *pre-tax* dollars. Why? It's simple: Your business generates income that you spend on expenses… and the remainder is subject to tax. So the money you spend on legitimate expenses comes from pre-tax, not after-tax, dollars.

Think of it this way. You earn a $4,500 commission after a property you listed has sold. You decide you need a new computer so you buy one for $1,500. You now have $3,000 left; if you don't earn or spend another penny, you'll pay taxes on that $3,000 in income. But you won't pay taxes on the $1,500 you spent on the computer because you spent pre-tax dollars.

Why is that important? Let's take taxes into account. To make the math easy, let's again pretend that your taxes add up to 30%; if you make $4,500, you pay $1,350 in taxes. You would have paid $450 in taxes on the $1,500 you spent on the computer, leaving you with $1,050. By using pre-tax dollars, you saved $450 on the expense compared to using after-tax dollars. (And you only paid $900 on the remaining income of $3,000.)

In short, after-tax dollars are good – because *all* dollars are good – but pre-tax dollars are *great*.

All of which leads us to our main point. An effective tax plan:

- Allows you to earn as much non-taxable income as possible.
- Maximizes tax deductions and tax credits.
- Shifts income into later years and lower tax brackets.

Because here's the bottom line: Every time you spend after-tax dollars when you could have – through effective planning – spent pre-tax dollars, *you lose money*. The key is to implement plans and strategies that allow you to turn after-tax spending into pre-tax spending. That way you won't live a Groundhog Day scenario. With just a little effort, every year you won't find yourself saying something like, "Oh, jeez, if only I had known I could have set up a plan to deduct my son's $4,000 braces...."

What kinds of tax plans and strategies? We'll take a look – but first let's ease any fears or concerns you might have.

Mistake #2
Audit Paranoia

Although most people do, there is no reason to fear the IRS. You should *respect* the IRS, but fear them? No.

Why? The IRS isn't out to get you. The IRS just wants you to follow the rules. Granted, sometimes the rules are difficult to understand... but it's *our* job to understand them; it's *our* job to be tax experts. (It's your job to sell houses.) We help you follow the rules.

With that said, some people should fear the possibility of an audit. (Some people, sure, but not you.) As you know, planning to *avoid* taxes is legal; planning or taking steps to *evade* taxes is not. The difference is based on fraudulent intent on the part of the taxpayer; in basic terms, you commit fraud if you know you are cheating on your taxes.

Here's what the IRS typically considers, in general terms, fraudulent:

- **Failing to report income:** Wages, income, tips, dividends, interest… or in small business terms, if a restaurant owner fails to report some percentage of receipts.

- **Claiming fictitious or improper deductions:** Overstating travel expenses, claiming a family meal as a business expense, or claiming fictitious charitable deduction.

- **Failing to keep adequate records:** Missing receipts, lack of backup for auto expenses, discrepancies between tax returns and financial statements.

Take care of the basics and you have nothing to fear.

So respect the IRS? Absolutely. Fear them? Never – especially if you have nothing to hide.

Let's take the subject of audits a step farther. Many people – even if they have nothing to hide – are still afraid of being audited. (The word does *sound* scary, I admit.) While getting audited can be a hassle, the typical audit consists of answering questions and providing backup information for certain items the

IRS questions. Full audits are fairly uncommon and have become even rarer in recent years.

How rare? Only about 1% of all returns are audited. That means your chances of being audited are 1 in 100 – but wait, there's more! Over half of those audits involved people filing for the Earned Income Tax Credit, a tax break designed to assist low-income working families. So unless you claim the EITC, your odds of getting audited are decreased significantly.

And like any good infomercial, there's still more: The IRS primarily targets sole proprietorships and cash industries like restaurants and laundromats – in other words, businesses that can fairly easily hide income and skim off a portion of their profits. (After all, a sale isn't a sale if cash changed hands and the sale isn't recorded and reported.)

What does that mean to you? Follow the rules – again, we'll help you do that – and you have nothing to fear. And if you want to avoid the hassle of a random audit, keep in mind if you currently operate as a sole proprietorship, your chances of getting audited are greater than if you change your ownership structure to a corporation (which we'll look at in detail in a bit.) If you're a corporation, you have a less than .5% chance of getting audited. So consider changing your corporate structure to reduce the chances of audit (and to take advantage of other tax breaks, too.)

So what are you afraid of?

Mistake #3
Operating as
the Wrong Business Entity

Discussing sole proprietorships and corporations leads us to another common tax planning mistake agents make. Most agents – and business owners – start as sole proprietors, then, as they grow, some set up a Limited Liability Company (LLC) or a corporation to help protect them from business liability.

Protection from liability is a great reason to change corporate structure, but choosing the right business identity can let you benefit from tax advantages, too. Even if operating as a sole proprietorship made perfect sense at one point, that structure may no longer be as effective – and may keep you from reducing your taxes to the fullest extent.

Let's take a quick look at the different types of corporate structure. My goal isn't to make you an expert; I just want you to understand the basics so you can make informed decisions. (And possibly help you sound a little smarter at parties.)

Legally speaking it's easy to start a company. If you start a company, your firm is by default a sole proprietorship or partnership if you don't formally opt for another structure. (As a real estate agent, you're unlikely to be involved in a partnership.) If you don't opt for another structure the business is not considered distinct and separate from you; you *are* the business, and you report any income on your personal tax return.

That's a simple way to start and operate a business, but it also has its drawbacks. Since you are the business you carry unlimited liability for any business debts. And if you're sued the result may not just cost you the company but everything else you own, too. (Ouch.)

If you want to limit your liability – in other words, limit your liability to what you have invested in the company – you'll set up an LLC or a corporation. (But, just to be perfectly clear, creditors may be able to "pierce the corporate veil" – feel free to whip that phrase out at parties – in cases of fraud or when legal and reporting requirements haven't been met.) And setting up a corporation can also help you lower taxes.

When you take liability and tax ramifications into account, setting up a corporation makes perfect sense – and failing to do so is an extremely common mistake many real estate agents make.

So let's look at your options. The main decision you'll make is whether you want to pay taxes on profits before they are distributed to you (in the form of wages) or if you want the profits to flow straight through to your tax return.

Limited Liability Company

An LLC blends the structure of a partnership with the liability protection enjoyed by a corporation. Many lawyers recommend that small business owners form LLCs because an LLC is relatively easy to set up and provides a fair amount of flexibility. (Keep in mind the average lawyer isn't necessarily concerned with reducing taxes, though.)

An LLC is like a partnership because the profits "pass through" to the owner's tax return. And you can use losses to offset other income, but only up to the amount you have invested; that's called the "basis." (In simple terms, that means you can't use a small investment to shelter a lot of income.)

Subchapter C Corporation

A C-Corp (that's what accountants and lawyers call it) is a basic type of corporation that does offer liability protection, but the tax rates are relatively high. The benefit of a C-Corp is that shares can be freely traded among an unlimited number of owners, which makes it a great vehicle for a small company about to go public. A C-Corp files its own tax return and distributes any profits to the owner. Those profits are in effect double-taxed since the corporation pays taxes on profits first and then the owner pays taxes, in the form of income tax, on any distributions. (Keep in mind to avoid double taxation "profits" can be distributed as wages, too.) Setting up a C-Corp isn't necessarily a good idea for a real estate agent but it could be a great choice for small businesses that intend to reinvest profits in the business...and hopefully someday go public.

Subchapter S Corporation

An S-Corp avoids double taxation, provides liability protection, and offers other benefits as well. S-Corps limit ownership to no more than 100 shareholders and those shareholders all must own one class of stock. (And that, for a real estate agent, is fine since in most cases you or your family will be the sole shareholders.) In S-Corps income flows through to the individual shareholders and taxes are paid at the owner level.

So why does all this matter, in tax terms? If you operate your business as a sole proprietorship or a single-member LLC taxed as a sole proprietorship, you may be paying as much in self-employment tax as you do in income tax. If that's the case, setting up an S-Corp will help you reduce that tax.

Here's why. If you're taxed as a sole proprietor you report your net income on Schedule C of your tax return. Your tax rate is based on whatever your personal rate is for that year. But, you'll also pay a self-employment tax of 13.3% on the first $113,700 of "net self employment income" (that's what the IRS calls it) and 2.9% on any income above $113,700. You'll pay an extra 0.9% on any self-employment income above $200,000 (if you file singly) or $250,000 (if you and your spouse file jointly).

Ouch. (Or should I say, "double ouch"?)

What is self-employment tax? Self-employment tax is intended to replace the Social Security and Medicare taxes your employer would have withheld and paid if you weren't self-employed.

Here's an example. Say your profit this year is $80,000. You'll pay taxes on that amount at your regular rate – that rate depends, of course, on your other income, deductions, credits, etc. *That* tax you can't avoid.

But, you'll also pay about $10,000 in self-employment tax. That tax you *can* avoid if you set up an S-Corp.

Here's how it works. An S-Corp is a special corporation taxed like a partnership. The corporation pays you a reasonable wage for the work you do. (You determine that wage; it's based, of course, on how much the company earns. You can't decide to pay yourself more than the corporation – meaning you – brings in.) If there is any profit left over, those profits pass through to you and you pay tax on that income on your personal tax return.

In effect the S-Corp splits your earnings into two parts: Salary and income. Again, salary is the wage you pay yourself, and income is the profit left over at the end of the year.

That division of earnings is what makes an S-Corp is so attractive. You'll pay the same tax on your wages as you would on self-employment income if you operated as a sole proprietorship. But you *won't* pay self-employment or Social Security tax on the income you receive.

Here's an example. Say you're a sole proprietor and you make $80,000. Your self-employment tax is $9,826. That leaves $70,174. Not bad.

Now say you've set up an S-Corp and you make the same $80,000. If you take $40,000 as salary, you'll pay $4,913 to Social Security and Medicare (FICA). But you won't owe self-employment tax on the income distribution of $40,000, which leaves you with $75,087.

Much better… because you avoided $4,913 in self-employment tax simply by changing your entity structure to an S-Corp.

And you can save that money every year. If we assume your earnings don't increase over the next twenty years – but I hope they do – you could put over $50,000 more in your pocket simply by switching to a more advantageous corporate structure that also offers liability protection.

What's not to love?

Mistake #4
Choosing the Wrong Retirement Plan

If you want to save more than the $5,000 limit for IRAs and defer taxes in the process, you have three main choices:

- Simplified Employee Pension (SEP)
- SIMPLE IRA (SIMPLE stands for Savings Incentive Match Plan for Employees... which is a great reason to use the SIMPLE acronym from here on out)
- Full-blown 401(k)

Just like with our discussions of corporate structure, my goal isn't to make you a retirement plan expert. Instead my goal is to help you determine if the plan you have is right for *you*... or whether you should set up a plan better suited for your individual needs.

While retirement planning may seem complicated, don't worry – it's not. I'll boil each form of retirement investing down to the bare essentials. The key is to make your hard-earned dollars go as far as possible towards providing you with a great retirement – and help you avoid looking back and thinking, "Oh, jeez, if only I had just…"

Simplified Employee Pension (SEP)

We'll start with a SEP. The SEP is the easiest plan to set up because, in real terms, it's like a turbocharged IRA:

- If you're self-employed you can contribute up to 25% of your "net self-employment income."
- If your business is incorporated and you are paid a salary, you can contribute up to 25% of your "covered compensation," (which in effect is roughly the same thing as your salary.)
- The maximum contribution you can make in 2013 is $51,000.
- The money goes straight into employee IRA accounts. There is no annual administration or paperwork required.

Keep in mind if you have employees you will be required to contribute on their behalf, too. (Since its unlikely you have employees, that provision is in most cases a moot point.) But if you *do* have employees you are typically required to contribute at the same percentage for them as you do for yourself, but you may be able to use what is called an "integrated formula" to make extra contributions for employees – say, for example, *you* – who have a relatively higher income.

Advantages of a SEP: Uses pre-tax dollars, is easy to adopt, easy to maintain, and flexible to operate. For example, if there is no money on hand to contribute, you simply don't contribute.

Disadvantages of a SEP: The contribution is limited to a percentage of your income instead of a fixed amount. (So if you make $30,000, the most you can contribute is $7,500.) And if you have set up an S-Corp to limit self-employment tax, you'll also limit the amount you can contribute to a SEP.

SIMPLE IRA

If you have less than 100 employees, SIMPLE IRAs are just what they're called: Simple. You fill out a two-page IRS form, pay a fee, and off you go. (The biggest administrator of SIMPLE plans is Fidelity

Investments; their fee is currently $350 plus $25 per participant.)

Here are some key provisions:

- You can contribute up to $12,000 per year in pre-tax dollars. (If you're 50 or older you can make an extra $2,500 as what is called a "catch up" contribution.) If your income is under $48,000, $12,000 is more than you could put away under a SEP since a SEP is limited to 25% of your income.

- You can match contributions on a one-to-one basis up to 3% of total pay; for example, if you make $50,000 your company can match up to $1,500 of your contributions.

- Funds go straight into employee IRAs. You can designate a single financial institution to hold the money, or if you have employees, let them choose where the funds are invested. (Most people with a few employees tend to choose one provider just to keep costs lower.)

Just like with a SEP, you are required to provide employees with the same match or profit-sharing contributions you receive. Again, as a real estate agent that is probably not an issue for you... unless you decide to hire your spouse and/or children; then they can make SIMPLE contributions too – and you won't mind the expense.

Advantages of a SIMPLE: Easy to set up, easy to maintain, uses pre-tax dollars. A SIMPLE also provides an advantage over a SEP for a business earning less than $48,000 because you are allowed to contribute more total dollars.

Disadvantages of a SIMPLE: You must match at least either 3% of salary for employees who participate in the plan or 2% of the wages of eligible employees who do not participate.

401(k)

The final step up the retirement plan ladder is the 401(k). Most people think of 401(k)s as retirement plans for bigger businesses. But you can set up what's called a "solo" or "individual" 401(k) just for yourself *and* take advantage of all the benefits of a 401(k).

A 401(k) is what is considered a true "qualified" plan: You'll set up a trust, adopt a written plan agreement, and choose a Trustee. The paperwork is the downside; the upside is a 401(k) lets you contribute a lot more money, with a lot more flexibility, than either a SEP or a SIMPLE. (For example, your 401(k) can invest in real estate if you choose.)

Let's take a look:

- You and your employees can "defer" 100% of your pre-tax income up to $17,500. (If are 50 or older, you can make an extra $5,500 "catch up" contribution.)

- You can choose to match employee contributions, or make profit-sharing contributions of up to 25% of pay. That's the same percentage you can save in your SEP – but on top of the $17,500 deferral.

- The maximum contribution for 2013 is $51,000 per person, not including any catch up contributions.

- You can borrow against your 401(k), make hardship withdrawals, roll the plan over... basically enjoy any advantages allowed under a Fortune 500 company's 401(k) plan.

Advantages of a 401(k): You can contribute up to $51,000 per year – or more, if you're over 50 – and turbo-charge your retirement savings. And you – okay, your company – can match contributions! And if you like you can hire your spouse and contribute to their account, too.

Disadvantages of a 401(k): Plans are generally more difficult to set up and administer. But if you operate the business on your own, we can help you establish an "individual" 401(k) that requires a lot less red tape.

There's one additional step you can take if you're over the age of 45, make a significant income, and want to boost your retirement savings. Let's take a quick look.

Defined Benefit Plan

A Defined Benefit Plan (DBP) is sort of like a pension. While pensions aren't particularly popular anymore – especially with employers – if you make more than $100,000 a year and you're over 45 you can use a DBP to dramatically increase the amount of money you put in your retirement plan.

Keep in mind you have to have the cash to put into your retirement plan; if you're living from paycheck to paycheck, a DBP isn't right for you. (You'd be better off with a SEP, a SIMPLE, or a 401(k).)

But let's say you do meet the basic criteria. If you set up an individual DBP, the goal is to pay out a "target" amount of benefits once you reach the retirement age you specify when you set up the plan. You can base that target amount on:

- A fixed percentage of your average salary and income over your entire career with your small business, or on salary and income over a specific number of years near the end of your career.

- A flat monthly amount.

- A formula based on the number of years you have operated your business.

You or your company makes annual deductible contributions to your account in amounts that will fund your target level of retirement benefits: The bigger your target benefit, the more you have to put in each year to make sure the plan is fully funded and can pay out that amount. For example, if your target benefit is $40,000 per year – meaning you'll be paid $40,000 a year by the plan when you retire – you have to fund the DBP sufficiently to provide that level of income.

But there is a cap; for 2013 you can target a maximum income of $205,000. (The number gets adjusted each year to account for inflation.) That's not much of a restriction – if you can put in enough to fund a benefit of $205,000, you're doing incredibly well.

With all that said, the beauty of a DBP is that contributions can be made using pre-tax dollars.

The downside? You agree to make annual contributions of a pre-determined amount. If your income goes down you may struggle to meet the contribution amount. To maintain a little flexibility, consider creating a blended plan by contributing some funds to a 401(k) and other funds to a DBP; if your income drops, you can reduce the amount you place in your 401(k) without jeopardizing your ability to make pre-determined DBP contributions.

Another quick note of caution: Defined Benefit Plans require a customized plan, annual actuarial calculations (age, life expectancy, income, etc), and a yearly report to the IRS once your plan is worth more than $100,000. A DBP is a great choice under the right circumstances; we can help you take care of the calculations and the paperwork.

Mistake #5
Failing to Employ Your Family

Hiring your children and grandchildren can be a great way to cut taxes on *your* income by shifting it to someone who is taxed at a lower (sometimes zero) rate.

First the basics:

- Your family employees must be at least seven years old.

- The first $6,100 of earned income is not taxed. Why? $6,100 is the standard deduction for a single taxpayer even if you claim that person as *your* dependent. Then, the next $8,925 they make is taxed at the 10% rate (which means up to a total income of $15,025.)

The result? With a little planning and reasonable record-keeping you can shift a significant portion of your income downstream.

Legally.

Of course there are limits. For one thing, you have to pay what is considered a "reasonable" wage for services performed by a family employee. The Tax Court defines a "reasonable wage" as what you would pay a commercial vendor for the same service, after making an adjustment for the child's age and experience.

That's not as hard to calculate as it might sound. Think of it this way: Say currently you cut the grass at your office. (I won't ask why your landlord isn't providing that service.) You decide to hire your son to do the job for you. If a landscaping service would charge $20 per cutting, it's reasonable to pay your son the same amount since cutting grass is relatively unskilled labor.

Or say you prepare newsletter mailings once a month. Hiring your son to apply labels and stamps frees you up to do other things; it's reasonable to pay him the $10 or so a temp service would charge to do the same work.

Now say your son has decent math and organizational skills; you may decide to hire him to help keep your books, organize your files, etc. Depending on the work you have him do, the skills required by a professional who provides the same service might command a higher wage. Since your son isn't a professional bookkeeper, pay him 20% less than you would a bookkeeper; that should easily be considered "reasonable." (If you're in doubt about what a reasonable wage for a particular job is, call and we'll provide guidance.) Or if he updates your website with new properties you've recently listed, pay him a little less than you would pay a web designer.

Hiring your son, like in these examples, accomplishes several important things. One, any unskilled work your son can take off your plate frees you up to do more important work: Showing houses, prospecting for listings, building professional relationships – in other words, *making money*. (Is your time better spent affixing stamps or showing a house to a potential buyer?)

And three – and from a tax perspective, most importantly – you may not be "out" some of the money you pay in wages. Here's why.

While you do have to deposit the paycheck in an account registered in your son's name, you don't have to give up control of those funds. If you wish, the account could be a Roth IRA. (If today you stick $1,000 in your 15 year-old son's account and it earns an average of 8% it will be worth over $46,000 when he turns 65.)

(While we're on the subject, here's another quick Roth IRA note. If he makes less than $6,100, a Roth IRA is the way to go; while Roth contributions are normally made using post-tax dollars, your son doesn't pay any taxes anyway because he doesn't make enough… so in effect his contribution is "pre-tax" and later he won't have to pay any taxes on the extra $45,000 he made in interest. Believe me – he'll thank you later.)

Digression over; let's get back to the funds you place in his account. Instead of creating a Roth IRA, you could contribute to a 529 college savings plan. Or you could set up a custodial savings account you control until he's 21. While you can't use the money in the account for things like food, you *can* use funds in a custodial account to pay for things that aren't "obligations of parental support" like private or parochial school tuition. (Those aren't considered "obligations" because he can go to public school instead.) Or you can use those funds for a variety of other purposes.

Here's an example. Next year you plan to send your son to soccer camp. The cost is $500. Under normal circumstances you'll pay the $500 with after-tax dollars, since soccer camp expense isn't an allowed business deduction. The cost to you? $500, in after-tax dollars.

But instead let's say he now works for you. Deposit his checks into a custodial account and when it's time to go to camp write the check. The end result? The camp just became, in effect, a business expense, and you paid for it using *pre-tax* dollars. If you lose 30% of your income to taxes, the camp effectively only cost $350.

And your son learned the value of hard work.

Keep in mind if your business isn't incorporated you are not required to withhold for Social Security until a child turns 18. (But you will be required to issue a W-2 so they can file taxes.) If you are incorporated, you will have to withhold Social Security… but if you took the money as personal wages instead, you'd pay Social Security tax anyway.

You are also required to keep reasonable records. The simplest way is to create a timesheet and record the hours worked and the type of work performed. You can take it a step farther by creating a written job description defining the duties involved – that way, if you're audited (even though, as you know, the odds of getting audited are pretty slim), you can back up the skills required to perform the job and why the wage you paid was reasonable.

So while there is a little hassle involved, employing your family is painless compared to the taxes you'll pay if you make this common mistake. Think of tasks you currently perform that keep you from your main role – making money – and "outsource" those tasks to your family.

Who knows; working together might not just be profitable, it might also be fun.

Mistake #6
Missing Out on Medical Benefits

What is the biggest concern for small business owners, sole proprietors… basically anyone in business?

The rising cost of health care… and the rising cost of health benefits.

Here's something I feel sure you know: If you pay for your own health insurance you can deduct it as an adjustment to income on your tax return. And if you itemize deductions you can deduct any un reimbursed medical and dental expenses… as long as they total more than 10% of your adjusted gross income. (Most people don't spend nearly that much on medical and dental bills, though.)

Or, if your broker provides group health care, the portion you contribute to pay for benefits is tax-deductible. Un-reimbursed expenses? Umm, not so much.

Here's what you probably *don't* know. With a little planning – there's that word again – you can write off medical bills as business expenses and pay those expenses using pre-tax instead of after-tax dollars.

How? Simple: By setting up a Medical Expense Reimbursement Plan (MERP) or Section 105 Plan.

A MERP is an employee benefit plan; that means it requires an employee in order to be valid. If you operate your business as a sole proprietorship, partnership, LLC, or S-Corp, you're considered self-employed. You're not an employee. So if you're married, hire your spouse and you're good to go. If you're not married, you can qualify by setting up a C-Corp.

But you don't have to be incorporated: You can set up a MERP as a sole proprietor or LLC simply by hiring your spouse.

(The one exception is the S-Corp. If you own more than 2% of the stock, you and your spouse are both considered self-employed for purposes of this rule.

You'll need to use another source of income, not taxed as an S-Corp, as the basis for this plan.)

Why hire your spouse? You need an employee to make the plan work; your spouse can be that employee. Employees covered under a MERP can be reimbursed for any medical expenses incurred by themselves, their spouse, and their children. So even though you're considered self-employed, your expenses *can* qualify because you're the spouse of an employee: Your wife or husband.

Complicated? Quick example: You're a real estate agent and you're operating as an LLC. Because of that you're considered to be self-employed. So you hire your husband. Even if he has another job in this case he's an employee, not self-employed… so he qualifies. Then, since you're his wife, you qualify as a spouse and your expenses are now deductible – and so are your kids'.

I realize it sounds a little convoluted, but that's how the tax law works.

And remember, the plan covers un-reimbursed medical and dental expenses. Say your health insurance covers 80% of a $100 procedure; you're still on the hook for $20. Under a MERP you can be reimbursed for the $20 you owe; the company in effect pays the bill using pre-tax dollars instead of the after-tax dollars you would have spent.

What expenses are covered? Here's a summary:

- Employee portion of medical and dental insurance (if the employer pays a percentage of the insurance cost)
- Co-pay and deductible amounts
- Major medical, long-term care, Medicare, and "Medigap"
- Dental care, braces, vision care, and chiropractor visits
- Fertility treatments
- Non-prescription medicines and supplies (with prescription from the doctor)

As you can see by the list, if it's health-related it's probably covered.

And the power of pre-tax dollars comes into play. You're already paying for check-ups, prescriptions, emergency care... with a little planning you can easily pay with pre-tax instead of after-tax dollars and reduce the damage rising healthcare costs does to your wallet.

So let's look at the basics of a MERP/105:

- You'll need written plan document (we can create one for you)
- No pre-funding is required; your company can reimburse you or pay the provider directly (either way using pre-tax dollars)
- The 10% itemized deduction floor for medical expenses is eliminated since you will no longer have to list un-reimbursed medical expenses as an itemized deduction
- Self-employment tax will be reduced because total income is reduced

As I said, you'll need a written plan document, which we can provide. You'll also need to track your expenses under the plan; we can also help you with that. But otherwise there are no special reporting requirements; reimbursements are listed as "employee benefits" on the company's tax return. As a result, you'll save on income tax and self-employment tax.

And unlike a Medical Savings Account or a flex-spending plan, you don't have to pre-fund the plan.

And you don't have to open special accounts. Plus there's no "use it or lose it" requirement like with flex-spending plans. Instead, a MERP simply allows you to legally avoid taxes by using tax planning strategies to categorize family medical bills as a business expense.

How does it work in practice? Say your husband needs to pick up a prescription. He can use his own money and the company can later reimburse him dollar for dollar. (You'll save all receipts, of course.) Or he can use a business credit card or business check and charge the cost directly to the company. Either way? Pre-tax dollars.

If you have non-family employees you have to include them too. (All employees must be eligible to participate in the plan; you can't discriminate in any way.) But there are exceptions: You can exclude employees under 25, who work less than 35 hours a week, who work less than nine months a year, or who have worked for you less than three years.

Most real estate agents don't have any non-family employees; if you do, that might make a MERP more expensive than you'd like since the company will be required to reimburse non-family employee expenses too. If that's the case and you offer health insurance to employees, you can switch to a high-deductible health plan and use a Section 105 plan to replace the benefits that are lost as a result of the switch.

So let's take a quick look at a Health Savings Account (HSA) just in case this applies to you. A HSA combines a high-deductible health plan with a tax-free savings account to cover un-reimbursed costs.

To qualify you'll need a "high deductible health plan" with a deductible of at least $1,250 for single coverage or $2,500 for family coverage. (That means if you're single your expenses must total $1,250 before costs start getting reimbursed. In this case, "high deductible" truly means *high* deductible.) And, neither you nor your spouse can be covered by another non-high deductible health plan or Medicare. The plan can't provide any benefit, other than very specific preventive care benefits, until the deductible for that year is satisfied. It's pretty restrictive.

Once you've established your eligibility you can open a deductible savings account. You can then contribute up to $3,250 for singles or $6,450 for families to that account. The account grows tax-free, and you can make tax-free withdrawals for qualified expenses like paying for most kinds of health insurance and for COBRA continuation or long-term care premiums. You can also use funds in the account for the same sort of expenses as a Section 105 plan allows.

Granted, the Health Savings Account isn't as powerful as the Section 105 Plan. There are specific dollar contribution limits and there's no self-employment tax advantage. But under the right circumstances, Health Savings Accounts can still cut your overall health-care costs.

We'll help you figure out which plan makes the best sense for your individual needs and circumstances.

Mistake #7
Failing to Deduct a Home Office

Just about any accountant will tell you: The home office deduction is probably the most misunderstood deduction in the entire tax code.

For years people were afraid the home office deduction raised an automatic red flag for auditors. But Congress has relaxed the rules and now it's far less likely to attract attention. And even if you are audited, as long as your ducks are in a row, why worry? Remember: Respect, not fear.

Let's start with a basic premise. Your home office qualifies as your principal place of business if:

1. You use your office "exclusively and regularly for administrative or management activities of your trade or business"; and (not or, *and*)

2. "You have no other fixed location where you conduct substantial administrative or management activities of your trade or business."

The rule applies even if you have another office so long as you don't use that other office more than occasionally for administrative or management activities. (So if your broker provides an office space but you almost never use it… you should be fine.)

Okay, that's a mouthful. Let's break it down into simple terms.

First, you have to use your office regularly and exclusively for business. "Regularly" generally means at least 10 - 12 hours per week, but that depends on the nature of your business. Since real estate agents spend a ton of time outside the office showing houses, checking out properties, networking… the key is that when you *do* need to perform clerical and administrative tasks, you regularly use your office for those purposes.

But if you only use the office a couple times a year, don't expect it to qualify.

And, your office must be used for business purposes only; if you use the space for personal reasons, too, it is not deductible. If your office doubles as a home theater or rec room, it doesn't qualify.

If you're only using part of a room you don't have to partition off your workspace in order to deduct it, even though partitioning might be helpful if you are audited. A desk in the corner of a room can qualify as a workspace as long as you count only a reasonable amount of space around the desk as your "office" square footage.

If you meet both those tests, it also helps to keep a log showing the time you spend in the office; that could provide helpful backup if you are audited.

If your space qualifies, start deducting expenses. (Sole proprietors use a specific form; if you've set up an S-Corp, there is no separate form required.)

Here's how you determine what you can deduct:

1. Calculate the square footage of your home office. If your office is a 10 ft. by 10 ft. room, then the total square footage is 100 square feet (10 ft. x 10 ft. = 100 square feet.) If you're only using a portion of a room, measure the space you are using and multiply accordingly.

2. Determine the total square footage of your home. (You should already know that number; if not, check an old appraisal or tax bill.)

3. Divide the area of your office by the area of your house. For example, if your home is 2,000 square feet and your office is 100 square feet, your home office takes up 5% of the total space. (100 / 2,000 = .05.) 5% is then percentage of your home expenses that can be written off under the home office deduction.

Now list all your home expenses, and start multiplying. You can deduct 5% of:

- Rent, mortgage interest, insurance, and property taxes.

- Utilities, repairs, garbage pickup, security, etc.

- Your home's basis (excluding land) over 39 years as non-residential property. (In other words, 5% of your home qualifies as a commercial property that can be depreciated.)

You can use home office expenses to shelter profits, but not to the degree that you end up with a loss. If that happens, you can carry forward those losses to future years to offset higher income. Here's an extreme example: Say your home office deductions add up to $1,500, but you only make $1,000 this year. You can offset earnings and carry the "excess" $500 forward to next year.

One caveat: When you sell your home, you'll have to recapture any depreciation you claimed or could have claimed after May 6, 1997.

And, you can still claim the $500,000 (that's if you're married; it's $250,000 if you're single) tax-free capital gains exclusion when you sell the home as long as the home office space was not considered a "separate dwelling unit," like a separate structure located elsewhere on the property.

The key is to accurately determine the percentage of your home allocated for business use, and keep a record of all home expenses that you deduct a portion of. Like any other tax planning strategy, keeping accurate records is critical.

Mistake #8
Failing to Maximize Auto Expenses

Do you take the standard deduction for automobile expenses?

(Do you even know what the amount is?)

The 2013 rate is 56.5 cents per; you can deduct up to 56.5 cents for every qualified mile you drive. (Keep in mind miles spent commuting to your office are not deductible; that's another reason to have a home office, because then you don't "waste" those commuting miles since your commute is as easy as walking down the hall.)

The problem is the standard deduction is truly *standard*. It applies to *any* car or truck – no matter how expensive that particular vehicle may be to operate.

Do you know what the total costs to operate your vehicle? You probably don't (at least not yet.) Fortunately AAA performs an annual evaluation of vehicle operating costs, taking into account gas, repairs, preventive maintenance, tires, licenses, and depreciation; here are the 2011 estimates (the results may surprise you):

Miles per Year	10,000	15,000	20,000
Small Sedan	57.6 cents	44.9 cents	38.4 cents
Medium Sedan	74.9 cents	58.5 cents	50.1 cents
Large Sedan	98.8 cents	75.5 cents	63.6 cents
SUV	98.5 cents	75.7 cents	64.2 cents

What did you learn? If you drive a small car about 15,000 miles a year, the standard deduction is possibly a little generous and may work in your favor. If you drive a large sedan or an SUV around 10,000 miles a year, the standard deduction doesn't come close to covering your costs.

What do you do if that's the case? If you currently take the standard deduction you can switch to using the actual expense method if you own your vehicle (but not if you lease.) And you can't switch from actual expenses to the mileage allowance if you've taken accelerated depreciation. (And if you don't know what that means, you probably haven't taken accelerated depreciation… or your accountant isn't doing a very good job of keeping you informed.)

But before we look at using the actual expense method, keep in mind one major premise: If you use your car in your job or business and you use it *only* for that purpose, you can deduct the entire cost of operation (subject to limits, of course). But if like most people you use the car for both business *and* personal purposes, you may deduct only the cost of its business use. We'll look at that in a second.

Calculating the standard deduction is simple: Total all your business use miles (which you'll know because you've kept a daily log of business use), multiply by either 51 cents per mile or 55.5 cents per mile, and add any parking fees or tolls, and any interest expense on your vehicle loan you paid during the course of business use. That's your standard deduction.

To use the actual expense method you'll determine what it really cost to operate the car for business use. You'll include actual expenses for gas, oil, repairs, tires, insurance, registration fees, licenses, and depreciation (or lease payments). (A quick note: If you're not familiar with calculating depreciation, we can help.)

If the vehicle is strictly used for business purposes you can deduct the entire amount. If you use the vehicle for business and personal use, first determine the percentage of use that was business. For example, if you drove a total of 10,000 miles and 80% of those miles were for business purposes, you can deduct 80% of the total expenses. And multiply away.

Then add parking fees and tolls that were incurred during business use, since those are calculated separately.

Now take a look: Which method saves you the most money? You are allowed to use whichever method is to your advantage – but keep in mind you are required to justify actual expenses if that's the method you choose. You'll need to save all your receipts and keep a log of the miles you drive for business purposes, including the length and purpose of each trip. (It's not hard if you take notes at the end of each workday.)

Again, you can use whichever method works out best for you – as long as you haven't taken accelerated depreciation. If you have, you can't switch from the actual to the standard method.

Mistake #9
Failing to Maximize
Meals & Entertainment Expenses

Good real estate agents entertain: They entertain clients, colleagues, potential sources of new business. Good real estate agents network. Good real estate agents build relationships – and few things help build a relationship like a nice meal or a joint social event.

But those activities are also expensive – and they can greatly impact your bottom line.

Unless, of course, you have an effective plan and you know how the tax code works.

The basic rule is you are allowed to deduct the cost of meals or entertainment having a bona fide business purpose. A bona fide purpose includes meals or entertainment with clients, prospects, referral sources, and business colleagues.

And tell me this – how often do you eat with someone who's *not* a client, prospect, referral source, or business colleague?

As a real estate agent, a profession where you're constantly marketing yourself, your answer to that question might be, "Never." As a result you should be as aggressive as you can – within limits, of course – in how you define a bona fide business discussion.

Hopefully you're aware the general rule is you are allowed to deduct 50% of your meals and entertainment as long as it isn't "lavish or extraordinary." (The dinner you have planned at Nobu in New York City might be a stretch.)

Why can you only deduct 50% of the cost? The IRS assumes you would eat, for example, lunch even if you didn't have a business purpose for the meal… so they compromise and meet you halfway on the expense.

So here's how it works. To qualify, meal and entertainment expenses must:

1. Be of a type qualifying as meals or entertainment.

2. Have a necessary relationship to your business activities.

3. Be supported by adequate records that substantiate the expenses incurred.

Now let's break those categories down.

1. **Be of a type qualifying as meals or entertainment.** In general terms, expenses for any activity intended to provide entertainment, amusement, or recreation can qualify. Examples: Entertaining guests at nightclubs or at social or athletic clubs; at theaters; at sporting events; or on hunting, fishing, or hiking trips. If a client is from out of town, providing meals, a hotel, or a car can also be considered an entertainment expense.

   Keep in mind tickets to entertainment are usually deductible but only to face value. (If you pay a scalper a $100 premium for Sooner tickets, too bad; you can't deduct the additional $100.) If you do not attend the event yourself but simply provide the tickets, you can decide whether to consider the tickets a business gift (deductible up to $25 of actual cost) or as entertainment (at 50% of cost.) And where spouses are concerned, you're usually covered, since when you're trying to sell a house the spouse is a client as well... so you can deduct permissible entertainment for both.

Entertainment expenses include the cost of meals you provide to customers or clients whether the meal alone is the entertainment or whether it's a part of other entertainment (like hot dogs and beer at a football game.) Meal expense includes the cost of food, drinks, tax, and tips.

And finally, you can deduct 50% of meals and entertainment at your place of business, at a separate venue, or even at your home.

2. **Have a necessary relationship to your business activities.** Expenses must be closely related to your business in order to be deductible. In the IRS's view, your expenses may qualify if they meet one of the following two tests:

   - **"Directly Related" Test.** If the entertainment takes place in a business setting (for example, the refreshments you provide at an Open House) and is designed to directly promote your business, the expense satisfies the Directly Related Test. If you can't meet the "clear business setting" requirement, the expense must meet *all* of the following requirements:

- You must have more a reasonable anticipation of deriving income or a specific business benefit from the meal or entertainment. (Wishing and hoping is not a reasonable anticipation.) But, you don't have to show that income or a specific business benefit was the result of the get-together – you just have to show you had a reasonable expectation there would be a result. (Fuzzy? Call me and we'll talk about it.)

- During the meal or entertainment you actively engage in substantive business discussions.

- The main purpose of the meal and entertainment is to actively conduct business.

With that said… what kinds of expenses tend to *not* be considered directly related? It can be tough to justify a direct relationship to business if there are substantial distractions like at a concert or the theater, or if you attend a cocktail party, or if the group includes people attending who are *not* there for business purposes. In other words, the clearer the purpose, setting, and participants, the better.

- **"Associated With" Test.** Meals and entertainment expenses may be deductible under the more lenient Associated With Test if they meet the following two requirements:
- The expenses are associated with the active conduct of your business.
- The meal or entertainment comes immediately before or directly after a substantial and bona fide business discussion.

Entertainment that occurs on the same day as the business discussion tends to automatically qualify as immediately before or directly after.

If the meals or entertainment and the business discussion *don't* occur on the same day, the situation is analyzed on a case-by-case basis. Mitigating factors can include where you went, what you did, whether you or the other parties are from out of town, and any other reasons the meals or entertainment didn't take place on the same day you had substantial business discussions.

Here's the key: Whether a business discussion is considered to be bona fide depends on the circumstances of each event. If you're challenged, you must establish you actively engaged in a business discussion for the purpose of obtaining income or another direct business benefit. Just keep in mind you don't have to prove you spent more time on business than on "pleasure." But you may struggle to justify four days of hotel expenses for one day of discussion.

3. **Be supported by adequate records that substantiate the expenses incurred.** The IRS requires you to keep accurate records showing income, gains, losses, expenses, costs... basically anything that affects your

income tax liability. (And you have to keep those records for as long as they may be relevant to any subsequent audits or investigations. In general terms, you need to keep all records that support items on your tax return for at least four years since the IRS can challenge your return for up to three years after the filing year.)

In order to claim any deduction you need to prove two things: What an expense was for and that the expense was in fact paid for. (In other words you can't fake a receipt or invoice.) What works: Receipts or invoices with a description of the item/service and its cost, canceled checks, and credit card statements or receipts.

If you're audited and don't have records of a certain expense but it seems obvious you must have incurred the expense (like, for instance, you ordered and received business cards but can't find the invoice), the IRS will typically estimate the amount of your expenses. But why estimate – and possibly miss out on deductions – when you can keep accurate records and deduct everything possible?

Certain expenses are subject to special documentation rules mostly because the IRS feels these expenses lend themselves especially to, well, cheating. If you don't have accurate records these expenses will probably be disallowed completely:

- Expenses for travel away from home (including meals and lodging).

- Meals and entertainment expenses.

- Business gifts.

- Automobile and other transportation expenses.

- Cell phones, computers, and other items that can be easily used for entertainment or recreation.

For anything listed above you need receipts for expenses over $75. For lodging you need receipts even if the cost was less than $75. (That may be a moot point; if you find a decent room for less than $75, let me know.)

And you have to substantiate the expense by showing the amount, the time and place, and the business purpose. Plus for entertainment, meal, and expenses, you have to identify the business relationship of the persons involved. (That's easy – just write names and purpose on all your receipts.)

For vehicle expenses, you need to keep a mileage log (a subject we already discussed.) Here's an important note: The IRS does not require you to keep a contemporaneous – meaning completely up to date – record of your expenses. But on the other hand, if you save receipts and make notes about time, place, participants, and purpose, your records will be as accurate as possible – and the likelihood is greater the IRS will accept them at face value. Recreated documentation looks and feels recreated... and raises a red flag for an auditor. Plus, if you systematically record your expenses, you'll ensure you don't let any slip through the cracks and you'll maximize your use of deductible expenses (and pre-tax dollars!)

So take a step back. How often do you entertain at home? Do you ever discuss business? If so, are you deducting the expense of those meals? You can deduct entertainment expenses if they take place directly before or after substantial, bona fide discussion directly related to the active conduct of your business. You can deduct the face value of tickets to sporting and theater events, food and beverages, parking, taxes, and tips.

So act like a reporter – but instead of "who, what, when, where, why, and how," record:

- How much?
- When?
- Where?
- What was the business purpose?
- What was the business relationship of the participants/recipients?

Then, if you're not sure whether an expense qualifies, give me a call – we'll figure it out.

Mistake #10
Missing Out on Expert Guidance

By now I think you can see that failing to create plans to minimize your tax burden and maximize your use of pre-tax dollars is a little like the story of Hans Brinker and the dike. No matter how hard he tries, he can't plug all the leaks and the water – or in your case, your hard-earned money – dribbles away.

So let's extend the analogy. If you come to us at tax preparation time, we can certainly help stick a few fingers in the dike and stop a little of the flow. We'll make sure you categorize expenses correctly, take advantage of any new or existing tax credits, and do everything possible to reduce your tax burden. In short, we'll help you make a bad situation a little better.

But what we can't do is rewrite the past. We can't look at your vehicle expenses and compare actual expenses with the standard deduction amount to determine which method saves you the most money… if you didn't keep receipts and records. We can't help you shift thousands in un-reimbursed medical expenses to pre-tax dollars… if you haven't set up an employee benefit plan. We can't help you avoid thousands in self-employment tax… if you haven't established the right corporate structure for your needs. We can't help you build a better retirement… shift income to family members… or deduct for all your qualified meals and entertainment expenses… if you haven't taken steps to put an easy to follow and incredibly powerful tax plan in place.

Here's the bottom line: You've probably heard the old saying, "Failing to plan is planning to fail."

Where taxes are concerned, this cliché is dead on.

Luckily, it's a problem that's easy to fix. We're tax *coaches*. We offer true tax *planning* – not reactionary, but proactive and individualized to your particular situation, needs, and goals.

We'll help you put together a tax plan that addresses the needs of your business, your family, your home, and your investments.

We'll even look at your last three tax returns to see if we can find savings you overlooked.

What we'll do – *together* – is make sure you keep as much of your hard-earned money as possible… by avoiding the common tax planning mistakes most real estate agents make.

And we'll have a little fun along the way.

Best wishes ---

Paul Dion

17943805R10044

Made in the USA
Middletown, DE
14 February 2015